The Endgame:
How I Escaped Ruin and Found Happiness

While every precaution has been taken in the preparation of this book, the publisher assumes no responsibility for errors or omissions, or for damages resulting from the use of the information contained herein.

THE ENDGAME: HOW I ESCAPED RUIN AND FOUND HAPPINESS

First edition. September 2, 2024.

Copyright © 2024 ZAHOUL LOVEN.

ISBN: 979-8227008015

Written by ZAHOUL LOVEN.

Table of Contents

"It is always possible to recover happiness and find the peace that we thought was lost. The force to change lives in each of us, waiting for the moment when that we decide to trust."

-Zahoul Loven-

Acknowledgements

I want to begin this book by thanking my support network, those who have been my pillar and my light in the darkest moments. Thank you for believing in me when I couldn't do it myself, for supporting me with your love, patience and understanding, and for accompanying me every step of the way on this road to recovery.

To you, dear reader, my deepest gratitude. You are the reason I dare to tell my story, in the hope that these words offer you comfort, guidance, and a spark of inspiration to keep going. If my experience can help someone else find their way to a full, happy, and peaceful life, then this whole journey will have been worth it.

Thank you for allowing me to be a part of your journey, and for unknowingly being a source of motivation for me.

1. Introduction: The Game Begins

My name is Zahoul, I am 18 years old, and until recently I could say that I had a normal life, even a good one, according to many. I come from a family that has always supported me in everything. My parents are honest workers, people with solid principles, the kind of people who believe in the value of effort and education. My grandparents, although elderly, are still the soul of our home; they always have wise advice or a warm smile. My two younger brothers are my inspiration and, although they sometimes drive me crazy, I would give anything for them.

I grew up surrounded by love and affection, and I never lacked anything essential. Sure, we weren't rich, but we didn't need to be either. My dad always said that being rich wasn't about having money, but about having a family like ours. And I believed him. I had many dreams: studying engineering, creating something that would really impact the world, traveling and seeing places, living life to the fullest. I considered myself a lucky boy, a good boy. And maybe that's why I never imagined that, in just one night, everything could start to change.

That night had been long. I had just finished a shift at the store where I had worked since I was 15; I never minded working, on the contrary, it made me feel useful, part of something bigger. One of my friends, Mauricio, asked me out. He told me he wanted to show me something "fun." I didn't think about it too much. Mauricio was a nice guy, older than me, someone I trusted. However, when he told me we were going to a casino, I felt a pang in my stomach. I had never set foot in one, I wasn't even interested in them. But Mauricio insisted: "

—-Come on, Zahoul. It's just to pass the time, nothing more."

Entering the casino was like stepping into another world. The bright lights blinded me at first; the sound of the machines, the laughter, the constant jingling of falling coins, the excited murmur of the people... everything immediately enveloped me. I felt like a kid in a toy store, overwhelmed by everything I saw, but also fascinated. Javier smiled at me, and before I knew it, he had me in front of a blackjack table.

—Come on, Zahoul, just one hand to try your luck —he said to me.

At first, I was hesitant. What was I doing there? I wasn't that kind of person. But I also had a curiosity, a kind of tingling in my hands, and an inner voice that said, "Why not?"

So I took some money out of my pocket. It wasn't much, just what I had saved up to buy a jacket I had seen a few days ago. I put the money on the table and sat down.

The first card I received was a nine. My heart started to beat faster. The next card was a king. The sum was nineteen. Not bad. I felt my mouth go a little dry, but I kept my cool. The dealer smiled and revealed his cards: eighteen.

I had won!

The feeling that ran through me was indescribable. It was a mixture of relief, pure excitement, and some kind of unknown pride. I felt a vibrant energy that filled me completely, as if I had found a new source of adrenaline that I had never known before. My whole body was shaking with excitement. It was as if I had touched a secret chord inside me. The dealer handed me the chips, and at that moment, the world seemed to stop. I could hear my own heart beating, the blood coursing through my veins. I felt that anything was possible.

I looked at the chips in my hand and for a second, I saw myself using that money for something more than just a jacket. I could help out around the house, pay some bills, buy my mom a gift, take my siblings somewhere special. The idea of making money so fast, of feeling that euphoria over and over again, started to seem like a good thing, almost noble. After all, I wasn't doing it for myself, but for those I loved the most.

That night I returned home with a smile on my face. I stayed up late, staring at the ceiling, still feeling the thrill of victory. I couldn't get the idea of going back, of repeating that feeling, of winning even more out of my head.

I told myself that there was nothing wrong with it. It was just a game, a small risk, and the worst that could happen was losing a little money, but nothing more. So I decided to go back. Just one more time.

But now, as I write this, I realize that something has changed. The visits to the casino have become more frequent, more intense. Every time I lose, I feel a desperation I never knew before, a need to win back what I lost. And every time I win, that initial euphoria is less intense, as if something deeper were taking its place.

Today I feel strange, restless. Something inside me knows that this is not just a game, that I am playing with fire. And the worst thing is that I don't know how to stop. Something is about to break, I can feel it. But I still don't know what it is, or how far this will go.

Help Section 1

This section provides practical tools and tips for those who are beginning to recognize the presence of gambling in their lives and want to take steps to control their behavior before it becomes an addiction. Here you will find some initial steps to identify warning signs and begin taking proactive action.

Tip 1: Recognize the early signs of addiction

Identifying the early signs of a possible gambling addiction can help you stop the problem before it develops fully. Some key signs include:

Bet larger amounts to feel the thrill:

✓ Feeling like small bets no longer give you the same thrill they used to.

✓ Constant need to increase the amount of money wagered to experience the same adrenaline rush.

✓ Experiencing frustration or boredom if you are unable to bet large sums.

Constant thoughts about the game:

✓ Spending a large part of the day thinking about your bets, strategies or plans for playing.

✓ Constantly checking your phone or computer to see the results of your bets.

✓ Diverting your attention from important activities (such as work or school) to fantasize about gambling.

Playing to escape problems or negative emotions:

✓ Using play as a way to avoid worry, anxiety or sadness.

✓ Gambling after an argument or a bad day, believing that gambling will make you feel better.

✓ You notice that you gamble more when you are stressed or emotionally vulnerable.

Tool: Keep a betting journal to understand your behavior

Keeping a detailed record of your gambling activities can be a powerful tool to better understand your patterns and behaviors. A gambling diary can include:

- Dates and times: Record every time you play, the time you spend and the frequency of your bets.
- Amount of money bet: Write down how much money you bet each time and how often you feel the need to increase the amount.
- Reasons for playing: Reflect on what prompted you to play at that moment. Was it boredom, stress, celebration, or something else?

Technique: "Self-assessment"

The self-assessment technique is a reflective tool that helps you analyze the impact of gambling on your life and make more conscious decisions. Take time to complete this exercise regularly:

Personal reflection exercise:

✓ Question: "What impact does gaming have on my personal relationships?"

✓ Please answer honestly whether gaming has affected your interactions with friends, family, or partners.

Evaluation of time invested:

✓ Question: "How much time do I spend playing compared to important or meaningful activities?"

✓ Write down the number of hours you spend gaming each day or week and compare it to other essential activities.

Financial consequence analysis:

✓ Question: "How has gambling affected my financial situation?"

✓ Review your bank statements, debts or savings, and take stock of how gambling has impacted your financial stability.

2. The Fall: Caught in the Trap

A few weeks passed since that first night at the casino. At first, everything seemed perfect. Every time I won, I felt a rush of euphoria that made me forget about my daily worries. My family was happy with the little gifts I had given them and I felt good about being able to help. But little by little, I began to notice that things were not that simple.

At first, the winnings seemed like a windfall. I didn't question it. But soon, I realized that wasn't always the case. My friend Laura, who also worked at the store, mentioned to me that she had won on a slot machine at a local casino. The thought of going back struck me, and I decided to pay her a visit. I figured that if I did it in moderation, there was nothing wrong. But what started as an occasional visit became a routine.

I remember one night in particular. I had won a significant sum in a game of blackjack, and the feeling was sublime.

I returned home with a new plan in mind: to invest a little in my future. I imagined using the money to pay for part of my studies and maybe save some for when I wanted to move out and live on my own. The plans were grand, and the idea of accomplishing them kept me motivated.

However, each time I lost, the desperation grew. The first time I lost a significant amount, I thought it had been an accident. Maybe I wasn't focused or just unlucky that night. But the losses became more frequent, and with each loss, the need to win the money back became more pressing. The euphoria I felt from winning was fading, replaced by a growing sense of anxiety and stress.

I remember one particularly rough night. I had lost almost all the money I had earned in weeks!

I felt trapped in a downward spiral. The lights in the casino no longer seemed so dazzling; the sound of the machines was no longer so cheerful. Everything seemed heavy, as if the air was charged with an oppressive energy. Instead of feeling excited, I felt exhausted, disoriented.

I decided I had to do something to recover my losses, so I started betting larger amounts. I thought that if I could recover my losses quickly, I could balance things out again. But the larger bets only led to more losses.

The feeling of desperation and the need to win became more intense, and the game stopped being fun.

The worst part of it all was that I started lying. To my parents, to my friends, to myself. I would say I was busy with work or that I couldn't go out because I had important projects. But the truth was that I was at the casino, trying to win back what I had lost. My relationship with my loved ones began to deteriorate. My siblings noticed that I was distant, and my parents, although they didn't understand exactly what was going on, noticed my increasing irritability and lack of interest in family activities.

One night, after a particularly painful series of losses, I decided I needed a break. I left the casino with my head full of dark thoughts, and found myself walking the streets of the city, aimlessly. The cold air helped clear my mind, but the anguish was still there, tightening my chest.

When I got home, I sat in my room and looked at the money I had won and lost in those weeks. The illusion of a bright future was crumbling. I began to question whether I would ever be able to regain my footing. The reality that I had no control over the game hit me hard. Every time I thought about going back, the desperation grew.

That night, I realized I wasn't alone in this. I felt like gambling had become something bigger than me, a force that was starting to rule my life. The initial euphoria had turned into a compulsive need, and gambling was no longer a fun pastime, but a trap I couldn't escape from.

As I write this, my mind continues to spin, and a feeling of unease washes over me. I know I've crossed a line, but I don't know how to turn back. The feeling of being trapped is overwhelming, and I'm not sure how much more I can take. Something inside me knows this is about to get worse. And the worst part is, I have no idea what to do to stop it.

Help Section 2

In this chapter, we explore how addiction can trap a person in a cycle of compulsive gambling, often driven by difficult emotions and situations. This help section provides strategies for identifying emotional triggers, building a support network, and using tools and techniques that facilitate recovery.

Tip 1: Identify the emotional triggers that lead you to gamble

Knowing the emotional triggers that drive you to gamble is crucial to breaking the cycle of addiction. Here are some common examples and what you can do when you identify them:

Work or academic stress:

✓ Example: Feeling a lot of pressure at work or school and turning to gambling as a form of escape.

✓ Action: Practice relaxation techniques, such as deep breathing exercises or meditation, to relieve stress instead of resorting to gambling.

Loneliness or social isolation:

✓ Example: Feeling lonely and looking for a way to fill the emotional void in play.

✓ Action: Stay in touch with friends or family, and seek out healthy social activities, such as joining a club or interest group.

Boredom or lack of stimulation:

✓ Example: Feeling bored and turning to gambling as a quick form of entertainment.

✓ Action: Plan activities that you enjoy, such as playing sports, learning something new, or spending time on a hobby.

Problems in personal relationships:

✓ Example: Having conflicts with your partner, friends or family, and using gambling to avoid confronting them.

✓ Action: Seek to resolve conflicts through open and honest communication, and consider seeing a couples or family therapist.

Feelings of failure or worthlessness:

✓ Example: Feeling like you're not good enough and using gaming as a form of validation.

✓ Action: Develop a routine of positive affirmations and work on your self-esteem with the help of a therapist or coach.

Technique: "Mindfulness" - Breathing exercise to manage anxiety

Practicing mindfulness can be a powerful tool for managing gaming-related anxiety. Here are three breathing exercises you can practice:

1. Deep 4-7-8 breathing:
   - How to do it: Inhale for a count of 4, hold for a count of 7, and exhale for a count of 8. Repeat this cycle 3 to 5 times.
   - Benefit: Calms the nervous system and reduces the urge to act impulsively.
2. Breathing :
   - How to do it: Place one hand on your chest and one on your abdomen. Inhale deeply through your nose, making sure your abdomen expands more than your chest. Exhale slowly through your mouth.
   - Benefit: Relieves anxiety by focusing the mind on the act of breathing.
3. Body scan with conscious breathing:
   - How to do it: As you inhale, focus on a specific part of your body (feet, legs, arms, etc.) and feel any tension or relaxation that exists in that area. Exhale slowly as you let go of any tension you feel.
   - Benefit: Helps connect mind and body, creating a state of full awareness that can reduce the desire to

ZAHOUL LOVEN

gamble.

3. The Background: Total Ruin

It's been ten years since that first night at the casino, and there's no doubt that I've walked a very different path than I imagined when I was young. Back then, I thought gambling was just a way to make extra money, an exciting way to improve my life. But what started as an innocent curiosity turned into an addiction that crumbled everything I had built.

At first, table games like blackjack were my main attraction. The sense of strategy and skill fascinated me. But over time, I found myself exploring other games. Slot machines caught me with their promise of quick and big rewards. And then, online gaming offered a way to gamble in the comfort of my home, without having to face the stares of others.

For the first few years, I managed to maintain a semblance of normality. I successfully completed my engineering studies, got jobs that, while not ideal, helped me pay the bills. For periods, I managed to stay away from gambling. I told myself that I could control the impulse, that I just needed a break, and then everything would return to normal. But those moments of control were fleeting.

As time went on, the need to gamble grew. Losses began to pile up and when I could no longer cover them with my own money, I started borrowing money.

At first, it was just to cover a loss here and there, but it soon became a constant practice. I borrowed from friends, from family, from anyone who could help me maintain the illusion that everything was under control. I lied to them about my motives, about my problems. I told them I was going through a bad financial time or that I needed the money for an important project.

The truth was that addiction had trapped me in a downward spiral. Losing money became an endless cycle: I would gamble to win back what I had lost, only to lose even more.

My financial situation became desperate. I lost several jobs due to my lack of focus and my increasing need to gamble. The promise of a bright future I had imagined as a young man quickly crumbled, replaced by a reality of debt and despair.

My family and friends began to notice that something was not right. Over the years my behavior became erratic: I started missing family gatherings and avoiding my friends. Small details of my daily life became excuses to hide my true situation. Concerned questions turned into arguments and eventually into a void of incomprehension. Everyone wondered what was going on, but I kept the secret well guarded. I didn't want anyone to know the truth.

I felt so ashamed and remorseful! I felt like I had failed everyone, including myself!

The debts grew to a point where I could no longer cope with the daily calls from creditors. Threats of legal action and constant demands for payment became a constant background noise. The pressure was overwhelming, and my world began to fall apart. Every time I thought I might find a way out, I realized I had dug myself a deeper hole.

It was at that darkest point that I began to consider the unthinkable. Desperation and a sense of failure pushed me to the edge. I felt trapped, with no way out, and the thought of ending it all seemed like a solution to my suffering.

I thought about the pain I would cause my loved ones, the legacy of failure and disappointment I would leave behind. It was a constant battle between the desire to end the pain and the hope of finding a solution.

THE ENDGAME: HOW I ESCAPED RUIN AND FOUND HAPPINESS

So with the last few bills I had left, borrowed obviously, I decided to try my luck for the last time, because if I recovered something of what I had lost I would continue with my life, and if not, I had already decided that I was going to end this suffering, end myself.

That night, I arrived at the casino with a mixture of despair and resignation. I knew I had no more money, but the urge to gamble was stronger than any logic. The lights in the casino no longer seemed so dazzling; the sound of the machines was no longer so cheerful. Everything seemed heavy, as if the air was charged with an oppressive energy. I felt completely defeated, with my head bowed and my hands shaking.

I made up my mind and placed the last amount of money on the machine. The game began. My face was disfigured, my heart was racing. The numbers were going down. I still had a hope, a small hunch, but no... Thirty minutes passed and I had lost everything, once again. But now it was all, there was no more!

I left the casino. I couldn't handle the guilt, the anxiety, the stress.

I decided to go to a park. I didn't feel like going home, I couldn't get there with the guilt I felt. I sat on a bench, lit the last cigarette I had, and until that moment I thought, the last one I'm going to smoke.

As I thought about how I was going to make my parents, my grandparents, my siblings understand what had happened, and not feel guilty when they found out I was gone, I began to cry, a little bit restrained, but I'm sure I caught the attention of some passersby, because at that moment, a figure appeared in the threshold of the trees. He was a middle-aged man with a calm presence, and he was wearing a leather jacket that gave him an air of authority. A small ray of hope appeared in my life. It was a combination of circumstances, an unexpected encounter with someone who understood my struggle and who offered me help. He looked at me with a mixture of surprise and concern, he slowly approached the bench where I was devising my plan, when I heard his voice.

—Hi, are you okay? —the man asked in a serious tone.

I didn't know him, but there was something in his voice that made me feel like I could trust him, even if just a little, I looked at him and replied:

"No, I'm not okay," I replied, my voice breaking. "I've lost everything. Everything I had."

The man introduced himself as Javier, a former professional poker player who had struggled with addiction for years. He told me how he had gone through a similar experience and how he had found the help he needed to overcome his problem.

"I know how you feel," Javier said with genuine empathy. "I've been there. What you're going through isn't easy, but there is help available. You don't have to face it alone."

I felt uncomfortable, but at the same time, desperate. Javier's offer of help seemed to be my only way out. Despite my reservations, I accepted his invitation to talk. It was a small, but significant step.

He went to a nearby coffee shop, bought two Americanos, and in less than 5 minutes we were chatting, drinking coffee, and I was much calmer. I told him about the last 10 years, the hopes I had for life, my addiction, and all the problems it had brought me.

These types of coincidences do not occur twice in life, that's when I began to believe that there is a higher power that takes care of us and sends us true help when we are in the most fragile moments.

He took me to a support group that same night, where I met other people who were struggling with similar issues.

That night, as I left the group with Javier, I felt a mix of relief and confusion. I knew I couldn't solve everything right away, but there was something about the conversation and meeting with Javier that made me feel like there was hope, however small.

That help was the first step toward recovery. I started attending therapy sessions, talking openly about my addiction, and looking for ways to repair the damage I had caused. I learned to face my problems instead of hiding from them. The struggle wasn't easy, but little by little I began to regain control of my life.

Today, as I write these words, I realize how far I have come. Although the road to recovery is still long and full of challenges, I am grateful to have found the strength to seek help and begin rebuilding my life. My story does not end here, but my hope is that sharing my experience can help others recognize the signs of addiction and seek the help they need before they hit rock bottom.

Help Section 3

This chapter focuses on the most critical moment of addiction, when all seems lost and despair can lead to the feeling that there is no way out. However, it is precisely in these moments of crisis that the turning point towards a better life can be found. This help section offers guidance on how to seek professional help, recognize that hitting rock bottom can be an opportunity to start over, and provides tools and techniques for managing high-risk situations.

Tip 1: Seek professional help if you feel like you have lost control

Recognizing that you need help is a brave and essential step in your recovery process. Here's how and where to seek help:

- **Where to look for help?**

✓ Addiction treatment centres: There are clinics specialising in treating gambling addiction. You can search in your area or at nationally and internationally renowned institutions.

✓ Hospitals and mental health centers: Many hospitals have psychiatric or mental health departments that offer addiction treatment.

✓ Support organizations: Groups such as Gamblers Anonymous, addiction-focused NGOs, or foundations may offer free or low-cost resources.

- **How to ask for help?**

✓ Take the first step: Go to your GP or a trusted psychologist and express your concerns. They can refer you to an addiction specialist.

✓ Make a call or write an email: You don't have to physically show up at a location to ask for help. You can start with a phone call or email to a treatment center.

✓ Ask a friend or family member to accompany you: If you feel uncomfortable, ask someone you trust to accompany you to your first meeting with a professional.

- **Who are the health professionals who can help you?**

✓ Addiction psychologists: They help understand the patterns of thought and behavior that underpin addiction.

✓ Psychiatrists: Mental health doctors who can diagnose and treat associated disorders, such as depression or anxiety, which often coexist with gambling addiction.

✓ Rehabilitation therapists: Professionals who work in treatment centers and help develop skills to cope with addiction.

✓ Addiction counselors: Specialists who provide practical and emotional guidance to overcome compulsive gambling.

- **What if I feel embarrassed about seeking help?**

It's natural to feel embarrassed or afraid to ask for help, but remember that addiction is a disease, not a moral choice. Professionals are there to help you without judgment. Think of asking for help as an act of courage and self-love. If you're embarrassed to talk in person, try sending a text or email first.

Tip 2: Recognize that hitting rock bottom can be the beginning of a new life

Hitting rock bottom can feel like the end, but it can also be the catalyst for profound, positive change. Recognizing this moment of crisis as an opportunity to rebuild your life is key:

- Accept your situation: Understanding that you have reached a low point is the first step to accepting the need for change.
- Visualize your future: Imagine what your life would be like without the burden of addiction. What would you like to accomplish? How would you like to feel? Use this vision as motivation.
- Surround yourself with support: Talk to people who understand and support you in your recovery process. Allow yourself to be vulnerable and receive help.

Tip 3: Create a support network

Having a support network can be a key pillar in recovery. Engage trusted people to help keep you on track:

- Friends and family: Talk openly to those you trust about your situation, asking for their support and understanding.
- Support Groups: Join groups like Gamblers Anonymous, where you can share experiences with others facing similar challenges.
- Mental health professionals: Consider seeing an addiction therapist for professional guidance.

4. The Tipping Point: Deciding to Change

The night Javier took me to the support group was a turning point in my life. The group met in a simple room, with chairs arranged in a circle. There was an atmosphere of calm and respect that contrasted with the chaos I had experienced in recent years. When we walked in, I felt overwhelmed, but also relieved to be there. The simple fact that I was not alone in this battle offered me some small comfort.

Javier turned to one of the group's coordinators and then came back to me. "This is where we start," he said, with an encouraging smile. "This group will give you the support you need to deal with what you're going through."

The first session was intense. We were asked to introduce ourselves and share our stories. When it was my turn, I felt a lump in my throat. My hands shook as I spoke, but the words came out of my mouth like a kind of release. I talked about my addiction, how I had lost control, and the despair I had felt.

"I feel like I've been in an endless darkness," I said, my voice breaking. "I didn't know who to turn to. I thought I was alone."

A middle-aged woman, who appeared to be one of the group's facilitators, looked at me with understanding. "Gambling is a disease," she said, her tone reassuring. "It's an addiction that affects your mind and your behavior. You're not alone in this. There are ways to manage it and begin to heal."

That moment was pivotal. As people shared their stories and offered support, I began to feel less isolated. I realized there was a path to recovery, and that I could take that path if I was willing to face my problems head on. The idea that there was a way out gave me a spark of hope.

The next day, I decided it was time to talk to my closest friends. Laura, in particular, had been a constant friend over the years. I found her at a local coffee shop, and asked her to listen to me. When I told her about my addiction, her eyes showed a mix of sadness and concern.

"I can't believe you went through all this," Laura said, her voice shaking. "But I'm here for you. I'm going to help you find the help you need."

Laura recommended me to a psychologist who specialized in addictions. Although I was relieved by the recommendation, the reality of not having money to pay for the sessions overwhelmed me. Laura, with a generosity that touched me deeply, offered to make the appointment for me.

"Don't worry about the cost," Laura said determinedly. "I'll take care of that. The important thing is that you start getting the help you need."

It was a gesture that showed me how lucky I was to have Laura in my life. Through her, I met the psychologist, who gave me the first step towards recovery. Her sessions were a refuge and a place where I could explore my feelings without fear of judgment.

It wasn't just Laura who supported me. I started to build a support network that included some friends and family. I decided it was time to be completely honest with my family. I gathered my parents, my siblings and my grandparents at home, and I told them the truth about my illness - I can now call it that too - and the difficulties I had faced.

"I'm so sorry I wasn't honest with you," I said, tears in my eyes. "I've been struggling with a gambling addiction and I've lost a lot." I didn't know how to tell you, but I needed you to know the truth.

My mother took my hand, her eyes filled with tears. "We're here for you, son," she said, her voice shaking. "It doesn't matter what you've done, the important thing is that you're seeking help. We're going to get through this together."

My father nodded, his expression serious but full of support. "We're going to help you out of this," he said. "If you need anything, don't hesitate to ask."

My siblings also expressed their unconditional support. Although there was a mix of shock and sadness at first, my family came together to offer me the strength I needed to face the disease.

The light began to shine again in my life. Support group meetings and sessions with the psychologist helped me understand the depth of my illness and develop strategies to manage it. Although the recovery process was challenging, the feeling of having a support team by my side gave me the determination to keep going.

As I write these words, I realize that I have taken the first step toward a better life. Although the road to recovery remains long and full of challenges, the hope of healing and rebuilding my life motivates me every day. My story is far from over, but I have begun to take control and move toward a future where addiction no longer defines who I am.

Help Section 4 : The Turning Point

This chapter explores the crucial moment when you decide to confront your addiction and take concrete steps to change your life. In this process, accepting that you need help, being honest with yourself and others, and seeking support in the community are essential steps. This section of

Tip 1: Commit to being honest with yourself and others about your situation

Honesty is essential in your recovery process. Being honest with yourself and those around you will allow you to receive the right help and build relationships based on trust:

- Be clear about your situation: Recognize your feelings, your behaviors, and the damage that addiction has caused in your life and in the lives of others.
- Share your story: Talk to people you trust, such as friends, family, or members of support groups, about what you're going through. Being transparent will allow you to release the weight of secrets and get the emotional support you need.
- Reflect regularly: Maintain a daily or weekly reflection habit where you evaluate your thoughts, emotions, and actions. This practice will help you stay mindful and committed to your recovery.

Technique: "Gratitude journal" (exercise to focus on positive aspects)

Using a gratitude journal can help you shift your mental focus from hopelessness to gratitude. This exercise will allow you to remember and appreciate the good things that already exist in your life, helping you to maintain a positive attitude throughout your recovery.

1. Set aside time daily or weekly: Set aside a few minutes each day or week to write in your journal. Do this at a quiet time when you can reflect without interruptions.
2. Write three things you are grateful for:
   - Example 1: "I am grateful for the support of my friend Javier, who has accompanied me in group meetings."
   - Example 2: "I am grateful for the opportunity to start a new day with the intention of improving."
   - Example 3: "I am grateful for having the inner strength to confront this addiction and take steps toward my recovery."
3. Reflect on each gratitude:
   - Think about what each point makes you feel grateful for. For example, how does your friend's support make you feel? How has starting a new day changed your perspective? What does having inner strength represent to you?
4. Include positive details and moments of improvement: Write

down any achievements, no matter how small, or any positive changes in your thoughts or feelings.

5. Reread your journal often: Use your journal as a motivational tool. Whenever you feel discouraged, reread the entries to remind yourself of what you are grateful for and to celebrate your progress.

5. Rebirth: Redefining Life without the Game

After hitting rock bottom and starting to seek help, the road to recovery was a mix of small wins and significant breakthroughs. Each step, though it seemed small at the time, contributed to a profound and lasting change in my life.

First achievements and small steps forward

The first few days after joining the support group and starting therapy were a whirlwind of emotions. The process of personal change was overwhelming, but also rewarding. I clearly remember the first small achievement that gave me a sense of hope: abstaining from going to the casino for an entire week, the week I began to open up to my family and close friends. It was a monumental challenge, but I felt a relief and personal victory that encouraged me to keep going. Each day without gambling helped me reaffirm my decision to change.

Additionally, I began to develop new routines that helped me stay focused and positive. I began exercising regularly, something I had never considered before my recovery. Not only did exercise improve my fitness, but it also lifted my mood. I remember the first time I completed a 5K race. The feeling of accomplishment and mental clarity I experienced after the race were invaluable. I felt stronger and more capable of facing life's challenges.

Wellness practices and new passions

Therapy became a crucial part of my life. I started attending weekly sessions with the psychologist recommended by Laura.

I remember my first therapy session with a mix of fear and mistrust. I was worried that I would be judged, that I would be labeled "crazy," or worse, that none of this would work. I entered the office feeling vulnerable, with a heavy feeling on my chest that made it difficult to breathe. But, fortunately, the therapist greeted me with a warmth I had not expected. From the first moment, she was objective and assertive, and, at the same time, she made me feel confident. There was no judgment, only understanding and a safe space where I could talk about my fears and frustrations without fear of being criticized. Little by little, thanks to her empathetic approach, I began to open up more, to better understand my situation and to take the first steps towards my recovery.

Over time, therapy became a place of learning and evolution, not only for me, but for my family as well. The therapist suggested family sessions, where my parents and siblings could express themselves, understand the nature of my problem, and receive guidance on how to accompany me in this process. This helped everyone feel safe and supported, knowing that we were facing this battle together, with the necessary tools to overcome each challenge. Feeling that my family was also being cared for and guided in a professional manner was an immense relief, and it strengthened us as a team in this new stage of our lives.

THE ENDGAME: HOW I ESCAPED RUIN AND FOUND HAPPINESS

Through therapy, I learned to identify and manage my addiction triggers. I implemented wellness practices, such as meditation and journaling, that helped me process my thoughts and emotions in healthier ways. A specific example of how meditation benefited me was the sense of calm I experienced after a session, which helped me stay focused throughout the day.

In addition to wellness practices, I began to explore new passions and hobbies. I rediscovered my love for music, which had been neglected for years. I began playing the guitar, which provided me with a positive and creative outlet. In my practice sessions, I felt a deep connection to my creativity that helped me stay focused and motivated. Music became a constant source of joy and self-expression.

Rebuilding damaged relationships

One of the most difficult aspects of my recovery was rebuilding damaged relationships. Two friends in particular, Marco and Diego, had been affected by my addiction. Marco had been one of the first to notice that something was wrong, and although he distanced himself at first, he was instrumental in my recovery process.

I decided to confront Marco and apologize. I found him at a café, and we sat down to talk.

"Marco, I know I've failed you," I said, sincerely. "My addiction has led me to behave in ways that don't reflect who I really am. I'm working on improving myself and becoming a better person. And rest assured, I will pay you back the money you lent me, in a moment of desperation."

Marco looked at me with a mix of surprise and understanding. "I appreciate you reaching out and wanting to make things right," he said. "We all make mistakes, but the important thing is to learn from them. I'm here to support you in your recovery."

This conversation was a first step towards rebuilding our friendship. Although it wasn't easy, Marco and I began to regain trust and strengthen our relationship. And although it took a while, 1 year to be exact, we set up a payment plan with which I paid him small amounts weekly until I covered the money he had lent me.

With Diego, the conversation was equally important. I had avoided talking to him for a long time, but I finally decided to face the truth.

—Diego, I know I've hurt you —I said, as we met in a park, because he had serious family problems and needed my support. He asked for it, but I didn't give it to him because I was involved in the casino—. My behavior has been unacceptable, and I'm working on changing. I hope you can understand that I'm committed to improving.

Diego nodded slowly. "I respect you for coming and talking to me. Addiction is complicated, but seeing that you're seeking help is a good sign. If you're truly willing to change, then I'm willing to give you a second chance."

These conversations were instrumental in rebuilding my self-esteem. While not all relationships were repaired immediately, the process of facing my mistakes and working on my recovery helped me feel more confident and rebuild my self-image.

Recovering self-esteem

As I progressed in my recovery, I began to notice an improvement in my self-esteem. Small achievements, such as staying free of gambling for weeks and establishing new healthy routines, contributed to my increased self-confidence. Music, exercise, and therapy helped me rediscover my worth and feel better about myself.

Looking back, I see how each step in the recovery process has been a key piece in rebuilding my life. Despite the challenges and obstacles, being reborn without gambling has been a transformative experience. I have learned to deal with my problems in a healthier way and to value the important things in life.

Regaining my financial freedom

Over time, I not only made emotional and spiritual progress, but I also found a job opportunity that allowed me to change my surroundings. I landed a job at a small company that valued my skills and offered me stability, something I hadn't had in a long time. This new job gave me the opportunity to start paying off my debts, although the road was not easy. Together with my support network, we developed a realistic payment plan , called a "snowball," and I began to explore alternative sources of income: I sold handmade products online, even opening a small home-cooked food business on the weekends. Although at first everything was uncertain and full of challenges, little by little I began to feel the satisfaction of regaining my financial freedom. Each debt paid off made me feel freer and more in control of my life, proving that, with effort and support, it is possible to overcome even the darkest moments.

As I write these words, I realize that although the road to recovery is still a work in progress, I have begun to find my footing again. My life is filled with new opportunities and meaningful relationships, and the future feels brighter than ever. Recovery is an ongoing journey, but each day brings me closer to the life I have always wanted to live.

Help Section 5. Rebirth

This chapter is about rebuilding your life after overcoming addiction by finding new ways to fill your time and mind with activities that foster well-being, personal growth, and sustained happiness. The key to rebirth is replacing destructive habits with healthy and productive practices, learning to enjoy the process of personal rebuilding, and using tools and techniques to visualize and achieve a better future.

Tip 1: Replace playtime with productive and healthy activities

Finding new activities to replace the time you used to spend gambling is crucial to staying on the road to recovery. Here are five examples of activities that can help:

1. Sports and physical exercise: Join a gym, take part in yoga classes, or simply go for a run in the fresh air. Physical activity releases endorphins, improves your mood and reduces stress.

2. Reading or a book club: Immerse yourself in the world of books or join a local book club. Not only will this keep you busy, but it will also enrich your mind and broaden your perspective.

3. Volunteering: Spend your time helping others. Participating in community activities or charitable organizations will give you meaningful purpose and a sense of connection.

4. Personal development courses and workshops: Enrolling in workshops on skills such as cooking, painting, music, or gardening can help you discover new passions and talents.

5. Meditation and mindfulness practices: Spend time each day meditating, deep breathing, or practicing mindfulness. These activities reduce anxiety and help you stay present and focused.

Tip 2: Learn to enjoy the process of personal reconstruction

The journey to a new life without addiction is not just the final destination; it is also a process full of discovery and growth. Here are five ways to enjoy this process:

1. Celebrate small wins: Recognize and celebrate every positive step, no matter how small. From resisting the temptation to gamble to completing a course or workshop, every accomplishment is important.

2. Set realistic personal goals: Define goals that are achievable and that excite you. Enjoy the journey of achieving them step by step.

3. Share your process with others: Talking about your progress with friends, family or in support groups will allow you to receive positive feedback and feel supported.

4. Write about your experience: Journaling or writing about your recovery process can be a therapeutic way to reflect on your journey and see how you have grown.

5. Find joy in everyday activities: Look for ways to find pleasure and gratitude in everyday activities, from enjoying a home-cooked meal to appreciating a walk outside.

Technique: "Positive Visualization" - How to imagine and work towards a better future

Positive visualization is a powerful technique that allows you to imagine and project a future filled with well-being and achievement, which motivates you to work towards those goals. Here's how to do it:

1. Find a quiet space: Find a place where you feel comfortable and free of distractions.

2. Breathe deeply: Before you begin, take a few deep breaths to relax and focus.

3. Imagine your ideal future: Close your eyes and imagine what your life would be like without addiction, visualize in detail how you feel, what you are doing, who is around you, and what your achievements are.

4. Use additional resources: You can use relaxing music, guided visualization recordings, or even a journal to write down your thoughts and visions.

5. Do it regularly: Dedicate 5 to 10 minutes a day to this practice, preferably when you wake up or before going to sleep.

6. Building a New Reality: Sustainable Happiness

Now, looking back, I realize that this whole process wasn't just about quitting gaming. It was about rebuilding my life from the ground up, redefining what it meant to be happy, and finding a deeper purpose than I'd ever felt before. I learned that happiness isn't a final destination, but rather a consistent path, one that involves making conscious choices every day to stay true to my values and my well-being.

Lessons learned and personal transformation

One of the most powerful lessons I learned was the importance of gratitude. At first, it was hard to feel grateful when everything around me seemed to be falling apart. Over time, however, I began to value even the smallest moments: a heartfelt conversation with a friend, a day without debt to pay, a laugh shared with my family. I learned to be grateful for things I once took for granted and to find joy in the simple aspects of life.

This mindset shift also led me to develop a renewed sense of purpose. It was no longer just about making money or achieving superficial goals; it was about finding balance and living a life with intention and meaning. I realized that I had the ability to create a positive impact, not only in my life, but in the lives of others as well. I decided to get involved in support groups for people with addictions, sharing my story and helping others see that there is light at the end of the tunnel.

Resilience to accept losses and strengthen bonds

Accepting that some friendships and bonds were irreparably broken was one of the most painful aspects of my recovery. Understanding that not everyone would be there for me was a hard, but necessary, lesson.

At first, I felt devastated and guilty, but over time, I understood that true resilience is not trying to keep everything the same, but embracing change and adapting to it. Those people who distanced themselves did what they felt was best for them, and that is something I had to respect as well.

On the other hand, the bonds that remained became stronger. My parents, my grandparents, my siblings, friends like Marco and Laura, demonstrated a patience and unconditional love that I will never forget. Instead of clinging to what I had lost, I focused on strengthening these relationships, building trust through honesty and transparency. I began to value sincere connections much more, those that did not depend on appearances, but on true mutual understanding and acceptance.

Staying on the road to recovery and helping others

I realized that recovery is not a destination, but rather an ongoing journey. Every day is an opportunity to reaffirm my commitment to myself. I realized that to stay on track, I needed to continue working on my emotional, physical, and spiritual well-being. I continued with my therapy, continued attending support meetings, and cultivated self-care habits that helped me stay focused.

Additionally, I felt a deep responsibility to help others who were going through similar challenges. I decided to become a mentor for new members in the support group, sharing my experience and offering a helping hand. I realized that by helping others, I was also helping to strengthen my own commitment to recovery. Hearing their stories, their struggles, and their triumphs inspired me to keep going and reminded me that I was not alone.

Building sustainable happiness

The happiness I feel today is not the euphoric, fleeting happiness I used to seek in gambling. It is a more serene, deeper, and much more sustainable happiness. I have learned that life can be unpredictable, and that there will be difficult moments, but I have also discovered that I have the inner strength to face those moments with resilience and dignity.

Today, I am aware of my limits and my strengths. I have learned to say no when necessary, to take care of my well-being before anything else, and to value each day as a new opportunity to grow. Don't get me wrong: there are difficult days, but the difference is that now I know how to face them without resorting to old destructive habits.

I have found new passions and renewed old hobbies. I have learned to love life without strings attached, to enjoy every moment and to live with a sense of purpose. My road to recovery continues, and I will always continue to learn, but for the first time in a long time, I can confidently say that I have found true happiness, a happiness that comes from within.

This rebirth not only saved my life, but also gave me a new perspective to fully enjoy it. Today, my happiness is sustainable because it is built on the solid foundation of self-love, gratitude, and the constant desire to be a better version of myself. I am here, and I am alive, and for the first time in a long time, that is more than enough.

Help Section 6. Building a New Reality

This chapter explores how to build a life that is not only free of addiction, but also filled with long-term satisfaction, purpose, and well-being. Sustainable happiness involves creating routines that foster mental and emotional health, embracing setbacks as part of the growth process, and using tools and techniques to improve our relationships and daily well-being.

Tip 1: Maintain a daily routine that supports your recovery

Establishing and maintaining a daily routine is essential to your recovery. A well-structured routine can provide stability, reduce anxiety, and create a sense of purpose and accomplishment. Here are five examples of how to do this:

1. Establish consistent sleep and wake times: Try to maintain a regular sleep routine that allows you to get enough rest. Getting a good night's sleep improves your mood, concentration, and ability to manage stress.

2. Schedule time for daily exercise: Dedicate at least 30 minutes a day to some form of physical activity. This can be a walk, a yoga session, or a workout at home. Exercise releases endorphins and improves your overall well-being.

3. Practice meditation or mindfulness at the beginning of the day: Start your morning with 5-10 minutes of meditation or breathing exercises. This will help you focus, calm your mind, and set a positive attitude for the rest of the day.

4. Organize your tasks into small, realistic steps: Break down your daily activities into smaller, more manageable tasks and prioritize what's most important. This will help you avoid feeling overwhelmed and keep a clear focus.

5. Include time for self-care and activities you enjoy: Make sure you set aside time each day to do something you truly enjoy, whether it's reading, cooking, listening to music, or spending

time with loved ones.

53

Tip 2: Don't be afraid of setbacks; they are part of growth

It is normal to experience difficult moments or setbacks during the recovery process. Don't see them as failures, but rather as opportunities to learn and grow. Here are some tips:

- Accept that setbacks are normal: We all face obstacles on the road to recovery; what matters is how you respond to them.
- Learn from every experience: Reflect on what led to the setback and use that information to strengthen your recovery plan.
- Seek support immediately: Talk to your support network, mentor, therapist, or recovery group if you feel like you're losing control. Don't wait until you're in a high-risk situation.
- Reset your recovery plan: Evaluate if there is anything that needs to be adjusted in your routine or coping strategies to prevent it from happening again.
- Be compassionate with yourself: Avoid blaming or feeling ashamed. Recovery is a process and self-compassion is key to moving forward.

Examples of wellness activities :

- Monday: 30-minute walk in the morning.
- Tuesday: Meditation or deep breathing session.
- Wednesday: Read an inspiring book or listen to a podcast.

THE ENDGAME: HOW I ESCAPED RUIN AND FOUND HAPPINESS

- Thursday: Call or meeting with a close friend.
- Friday: Time for a hobby (painting, gardening, cooking something new).
- Weekends: Longer or more rewarding activities like a walk in nature, a day of rest without electronic devices, or a workshop or class in something new.

7. Conclusion: A New Commitment to Life

Looking back, I recognize that accepting my illness was the first and most difficult step on my road to recovery. For a long time, I refused to accept that I was a gambling addict. I told myself that I could control gambling, that it wasn't that bad, that it was just a bad streak that I could overcome with more money and more luck. But the truth is that gambling addiction is not just a self-control problem; it is an illness, an internal struggle that takes root deep within us, seeking to fill a void that can never be satisfied that way.

Understanding this was key. I am not a failure or weak for having fallen into this trap. Addiction does not define who I am, but it did force me to confront my fears, my insecurities, and my emotional shortcomings. Accepting that I needed help, that I couldn't do it alone, was liberating. I was no longer ashamed of my condition; on the contrary, every day in recovery was a reminder of my strength, of my ability to rebuild myself from the ashes.

Message for others struggling with gambling addiction

If you're reading this and you're struggling with gambling or any other addiction, I want to tell you that there is hope. I know that sometimes it seems impossible to get out of the hole, that the world closes in on you and you feel completely alone. But believe me, you're not alone. There are people willing to help you, to listen to you, to walk by your side every step of your recovery. It may not be easy and you may have to face many shadows inside yourself, but you will also discover a light you never thought you had.

Find your support network, whether it's family, friends, or even a group of people you don't know but who have been through the same thing as you. Don't be afraid to seek professional help. There are tools, techniques, and strategies that will allow you to understand yourself better and learn to live without depending on that addiction that has caused you so much harm.

Be kind to yourself in this process; it is not a straight or perfect path, but every step you take is a triumph.

Celebration and gratitude

Today, after all this, I can say that I feel grateful. Grateful for the lessons learned, for the people who stayed by my side, and for the opportunity to live in a new, conscious and full way. The healing process has allowed me to know myself more deeply, to value those around me more, and to love life with all its imperfections...

...Laughter fills the small living room, as I look around and see the faces of those who have accompanied me on this journey. Javier, sitting next to me, pats me on the back and says with a smile, "Remember that time I met you in that park? I never thought you would end up being my best friend."

My parents, grandparents, siblings and close friends, like Laura, are here too, all gathered to celebrate my 35th birthday. It's a simple party, but full of meaning. There's home-cooked food, soft music in the background and a warm atmosphere in the air.

My mother, laughing, approaches me with a plate of food in her hands. "I can't believe we're here today, celebrating this," she says, her eyes filled with tears, but this time with joy. "I never imagined we'd get to this point after everything we've been through."

My "little" brother, now 30 years old, Carlos, jokes: "Remember when Zahoul said he was going to win everything back with his 'great strategy' in blackjack? What a genius!" We all laugh. It 's no longer a bitter laugh, but one filled with relief and happiness. Even I join in the joke. "Yeah, well, I can't say it was the best idea of my life..."

THE ENDGAME: HOW I ESCAPED RUIN AND FOUND HAPPINESS

Laura comes over with a drink in her hand and hugs me. Zahoul, you have come an incredible way. You have inspired so many of us, and I want you to know how proud I am of you."

I look at Javier and the new friends I've made at the support group. Some of them have brought their families along, too, people who are now part of my inner circle. Sitting on the couch, sharing stories, it feels like we've always been a family.

Finally, I raise my glass. "To all of you, thank you. For believing in me when I couldn't. For giving me a second, third, and fourth chance. For never letting go. I'm here today, stronger and happier, because each of you has helped me see life with new eyes."

Javier, always with his good humour, adds: "And to Zahoul's new bet... the bet on life!" We all toast and laugh.

That night, amid laughter, shared stories, and a deep sense of community, I understand that I have won something far more valuable than any prize in a game: I have won a new life, full of love, purpose, and gratitude. This is, without a doubt, the best bet I have ever made in my life.

Help Section 7. Conclusion

This final chapter focuses on the continued commitment to personal growth and the importance of sharing your recovery story to inspire others. Recovery is an ongoing journey that does not end with overcoming addiction, but opens the door to new opportunities for learning, service, and self-reflection.

Tip 1: Share your story to help others

Sharing your recovery story can not only help others facing similar struggles, but it also helps you stay committed to your journey. Here are some tips on how to do so:

- Find a safe space to share: Consider sharing your story in support groups, in your community, or at local events where addiction recovery is discussed.
- Be authentic and honest: Speak from the heart, sharing both challenges and achievements. Authenticity is what inspires others.
- Focus on the process and not just the result: Highlight the path taken, the lessons learned, and the tools you used to overcome difficulties.
- Use different means to share: Write a blog, create videos, or participate in podcasts where you can share your experience.
- Focus on positive impact: Share how your life has changed for the better, but also acknowledge persistent challenges and the value of staying on track.

8. Epilogue: Reconciliation with the Past and Projection into the Future

It's been a few years since that day when my life began to take an unexpected turn. Sometimes, when I close my eyes, I see myself back in that casino, with my breathing accelerated and my heart pounding, feeling the adrenaline of gambling. But today, when I think of those images, I no longer feel guilt or shame; I feel understanding, empathy for that lost young man who was looking for a way out, an answer to his concerns and fears.

Reflecting on my past, I no longer regret the mistakes I made. Yes, there were dark moments and wrong decisions, but it was all part of a necessary learning process. Today I am grateful for the path I have taken because, without those crooked steps, I would not have gotten to where I am now. I am grateful for every fall, every sleepless night, every debt that seemed insurmountable. I am grateful for those who walked away, because they left me space to find myself, and for those who stayed, because they taught me what unconditional love and friendship really mean.

I am especially grateful to the people who were a fundamental part of my recovery. To Javier, who saw something in me that I didn't even see myself. To Laura, who always encouraged me to seek professional help. To my parents, for their unwavering love, even when they didn't know how to handle my situation. To my grandparents and siblings, for being a refuge in the middle of the storm. And to myself, for not giving up, for getting up every day willing to fight a little harder, despite everything.

Projection into the future

Now, with a healed heart and a clearer mind, I have realized that my mission in this world goes far beyond my own recovery. My story can be a light for others, a sign that there is a way, even when everything seems lost. That is why I have decided to dedicate myself to helping those who are still in that dark tunnel of addiction.

I have begun to collaborate with foundations and support groups for people with gambling addiction, sharing my story in workshops and talks. I have also written articles, and this book, in the hope that my words will reach those who need it most. My goal is not only to show that recovery is possible, but also to destigmatize this disease, reminding the world that behind every addicted person there is a story, an internal struggle, and a deep desire to change.

But I also have personal dreams. I would love to found a rehabilitation center that not only offers therapy and support, but also provides practical tools for reintegrating into society, such as skills workshops, educational support, and financial advice.

I know that for many, reintegration can be as challenging as recovery itself, and I want them to find in this center a place of hope and transformation.

Personally, I have decided not to run anymore, but to enjoy every step, every day. I continue to work at my job, which allows me to constantly learn and grow. I continue to explore new passions, such as music, photography, and hiking, which connect me to the beauty of the world in ways I never imagined. And I keep my support network stronger than ever, knowing that there is no recovery without community.

Closing and gratitude

Today, when I think about the future, I see it with optimism and hope. I am grateful for the opportunity to live this second chance with the awareness of someone who knows what it is to hit rock bottom, but also what it is to get up and be reborn. I don't know what fate has in store for me, but I know that I have the strength, resilience and support necessary to face whatever comes.

This is just the beginning of a different path, one that won't always be easy, but will certainly be authentic. And if my story can help just one person find their way, it will have been worth everything I've been through.

So, to all of you reading this, thank you for joining me on this journey. Thank you for believing in me, for offering me your support, and for allowing me to share a little light in the midst of darkness. And above all, thank you to life, for giving me a new bet, one that I make today with love, with purpose, and with the certainty that, no matter what comes, I am already a winner.

Help Section 8 Epilogue

In this epilogue, the key is to find peace with the past and build a path toward the future filled with possibilities and growth. This helpful section provides tools for personal reconciliation, visualizing new opportunities, and planning for a brighter future.

Tip 1: Learn to reconcile with your past, forgiving yourself and others

Reconciling with the past is an essential step to healing and moving forward. Forgiving yourself and those around you doesn't mean justifying mistakes, but rather freeing yourself from the emotional baggage that prevents you from growing. Here are some suggestions to help you do so:

1. Accept your mistakes as part of the learning process: Understand that mistakes are opportunities to learn and grow. Instead of beating yourself up for them, identify what they taught you and how they made you stronger.

2. Practice forgiveness: Take time to reflect on the people who have hurt you and those you have hurt. Write a letter of forgiveness, either to yourself or to others, without the need to send it. This symbolic act can help you release resentments.

3. Focus on the present: Practice mindfulness to anchor yourself in the present. Remember that the past does not define your future, and that every day is a new opportunity to be the best version of yourself.

4. Talk to a therapist or counselor: Seeking professional help can be crucial to processing feelings of guilt, shame, or resentment. A therapist can guide you through the process of acceptance and forgiveness.

5. Create a releasing ritual: Develop a symbolic ritual to let go of the past, such as burning papers with negative thoughts or

ZAHOUL LOVEN

creating a personal releasing ceremony.

Technique: "Dream Mapping" - Exercise to plan an exciting and purposeful future

Dream Mapping is a visual exercise that helps you plan a future you're excited about by identifying your dreams and creating a roadmap to achieve them. How to Do a Dream Map:

1. Gather your materials: You'll need a large sheet of paper or a corkboard, colored markers, magazines, scissors, glue, personal photos, and any other materials that inspire you.

2. Define your areas of interest: Divide your sheet or board into sections, such as: "Health", "Relationships", "Career", "Personal Development", "Hobbies", etc.

3. Fill the map with dreams and goals: In each section, place images, phrases, or words that represent your dreams and goals for that area of your life. Be as specific as possible.

4. Put your map in a visible place: Keep your Dream Map in a place where you will see it regularly. This will keep your goals in the forefront of your mind and motivate you to work towards them.

5. Review and update your map regularly: Make it a habit to review your Dream Map every six months to a year. Adjust your goals as needed and celebrate your accomplishments.

9. Family Support in Recovery

Gambling addiction is a complex illness that profoundly affects not only those who suffer from it, but also their loved ones. Family members and friends may feel caught between compassion and frustration, trying to help while protecting their own well-being. This chapter is dedicated to guiding them on how to handle the situation calmly, be an effective support, and at the same time protect themselves from the effects that gambling addiction can have on their lives.

Understanding gambling addiction

Gambling addiction is a disease that affects the mind and behavior. It is important to understand that this addiction is not a lack of character, morality or willpower; it is a disease that manifests itself through an uncontrollable impulse to gamble.

The brain of a person with a gambling problem seeks the instant gratification that gambling offers, ignoring the long-term consequences. Understanding this helps family members not blame the person with a gambling problem for their behavior, but see them as someone who needs help.

How to keep calm

It's natural to feel frustration, fear, or anger when faced with a loved one with a gambling disorder. However, reacting with anger or pressure only makes the situation worse. Staying calm is essential to providing effective support. Some strategies for managing these emotions include practicing deep breathing, meditating, and remembering that the person is not actively choosing to destroy their life or relationships, but is dealing with an illness that is overwhelming them.

Ways to offer support

Offering support is not just about being emotionally understanding, but also about providing practical support. This can include:

- Accompany the compulsive gambler to therapies or recovery meetings.
- Get involved in recovery activities, such as support groups.
- Help manage finances to prevent the person from having easy access to money for gambling.
- Offer healthy distractions, such as physical or creative activities.

Effective communication

Communication is key to supporting a person in recovery. Speaking from a place of empathy and non-judgment is essential. For example, instead of saying, "Why can't you stop?" you could express concern by saying, "I understand that this is hard for you, and I'm here to support you." This opens up a space for honesty and connection, preventing the person from feeling attacked or shamed.

Take care of yourself

It's easy to forget that family and friends need care, too. A loved one's addiction can affect the emotional, physical, and financial well-being of those around them. Setting healthy boundaries, such as not lending money or not allowing the gambling behavior to control the family dynamic, is critical. Seeking outside support, such as self-therapy or family support groups, can be very helpful in managing stress.

Understanding relapses

Relapses are common in any recovery process. Emotionally preparing for them is vital to maintaining hope and patience. If a relapse occurs, try not to react with anger or despair. Instead, focus on supporting the person back on the road to recovery, recognizing that relapses are opportunities to learn and reinforce coping strategies.

What is a support network? How do they work? How are they formed?

A support network is a group of people who provide emotional, moral, and practical help to someone who is going through a difficult time. To form a support network, it is important to identify friends, family members, or professionals who are willing to listen and offer support without judgment. Invite these people to become involved in the recovery process, whether by accompanying you to meetings, participating in open conversations, or simply being there to listen.

Final reflection

Helping a loved one overcome gambling addiction is not an easy task, but with patience, empathy, and open communication, it is possible to be a valuable support without losing yourself in the process. Always remember to take care of yourself and seek your own well-being, because only from there will you be able to provide the support that your loved one really needs.

Help Section 9 - Family Support in Recovery

This chapter offers guidance and support to family members of people with gambling problems, providing practical advice, tools and techniques to manage the situation in an effective and healthy way. Recovery is a shared process, and this section will help family members contribute positively to the well-being of all involved.

Tip 1: Avoid confrontations during tense moments; choose quiet moments to discuss the situation

Talking about addiction is a difficult conversation that requires a sensitive and considerate approach. Confrontations during times of high tension can make the situation worse and lead to resistance.

- Choose the right time: Find times when the person is calm and relaxed to talk about their gambling problems. Avoid bringing up the topic during arguments or when the person is clearly agitated.
- Create a safe environment: Make sure the place where you talk is comfortable and private. This can make the person feel more open to conversation.
- Use constructive language: Use "I" instead of "you" to express your feelings (for example, "I feel worried when you play" instead of "you are always playing").

Technique: "Empathetic Listening" - Exercise to practice listening without judging

"Empathic Listening" involves being present and actively listening without judging or interrupting. This technique can help the person in recovery feel understood and supported. How to practice empathic listening:

1. Focus on the person: Give your full attention to the person speaking. Avoid getting distracted by your phone or looking at your watch.

2. Avoid interrupting: Let the person speak without interrupting, even if you feel the need to correct them or add something.

3. Reflect what you hear: Use phrases like, "My understanding is that..." or "It sounds like you're feeling..." to show that you're paying attention and validate their feelings.

4. Ask open-ended questions: Ask questions that invite the person to share more details about their feelings or thoughts (for example, "How did you feel at that moment?").

5. Express empathy: Use phrases like "I understand that this is difficult for you" to show understanding and support.

Tip 2: Don't make important financial decisions without consulting an addiction professional

Financial decisions can be critical when living with someone with a gambling addiction. Making them without proper advice can have adverse consequences.

- Consult a financial counselor who specializes in addictions: A professional can help you assess your financial situation and create a plan that protects both your interests and those of the person in recovery.
- Avoid signing guarantees or loans: Do not agree to sign financial documents without proper advice, even if you feel emotional pressure.
- Develop a family budget: Create a budget that includes the person in recovery so they can feel like they are part of the financial recovery process.

Tip 3: Reinforce any small positive achievements or efforts made by the person in recovery

It is essential to reinforce any positive steps that the person in recovery makes, no matter how small. Constant recognition can motivate them to keep going.

- Praise positive efforts: Acknowledge every effort they make, such as attending a support group meeting or resisting the temptation to gamble.
- Offer non-monetary rewards: Offer rewards like going out somewhere they like or doing a fun activity together.
- Be patient and acknowledge gradual progress: Understand that recovery is not linear. Appreciate the small steps forward, even if there are setbacks.

Tip 4: How to manage your own stress

It is important for family members to also take care of themselves in order to provide effective support without sacrificing their well-being.

Self-Care Techniques for Family Members

- Meditation: Spend 10-15 minutes a day meditating. This can help you reduce stress and find inner calm.
- Exercise: Practice physical activity regularly to release endorphins, improve mood and reduce stress.
- Talk to a counselor: Consider attending individual or group therapy for emotional support and professional guidance.

Dear reader

First of all, I want to thank you deeply for having come this far, for having shared this journey with me, and for having taken the time to understand a disease that affects so many of us in such different ways. I am convinced that there are no coincidences, and that you and I have found each other on these pages for a powerful reason: because there is a better life waiting for you, a full life, full of meaning, of healthy relationships, of inner peace, and of stability in every sense.

This book has been a guide to a challenging path, but also one filled with hope and transformation. The tools and techniques we have shared are not just words on paper; they are real, practical strategies that have helped many, including myself, to recover our lives from the abyss of addiction. I invite you to not only read them, but to put them into practice with courage and determination. Form your own support network; surround yourself with people who understand you, who push you, and who help you to be the best version of yourself. Don't be afraid to open up to them, to be vulnerable, and to accept their support.

Remember that you are not alone on this journey. Don't hesitate to seek help from professionals: therapists, counselors, support groups. They are here to guide you, listen to you, and help you find the strength you may not have known you had.

If at any time you doubt yourself, think about all the reasons why you are fighting: to recover your life, your fullness, to strengthen your relationships, to find the peace of mind you so deserve, and to build economic stability that allows you to live without ties.

To those of you reading this who are family or friends of someone in recovery, I want to say: Thank you! Thank you for being there, for providing unconditional love and endless support. Your presence is essential in this process. Continue to support them, continue to believe in them, and in yourselves as well. Rest assured that everything will be okay, because you are doing the right thing.

This book is coming to an end, but your journey to recovery and healing is just beginning. There is a beautiful life waiting for you on the other side, full of opportunities, laughter, new experiences, and renewed peace. Believe in yourself, take the next step, and keep moving forward, because every step you take is a victory.

Thank you again for being here, for reading, for learning, for fighting. Never forget that you have the power to change your life in your hands. And always remember: it is never too late to start over.

Go ahead! Everything you need is already within you.

With gratitude and hope,

Zahoul Loven

THE ENDGAME: HOW I ESCAPED RUIN AND FOUND HAPPINESS

I hope these words can inspire you and give you the energy you need to continue on your path of recovery or support. Everything will be great!

Don't miss out!

Visit the website below and you can sign up to receive emails whenever ZAHOUL LOVEN publishes a new book. There's no charge and no obligation.

https://books2read.com/r/B-A-FEXJC-RZFYE